ish

Short Walks
Bodmin Moor

Paul White

Bossiney Books · Launceston

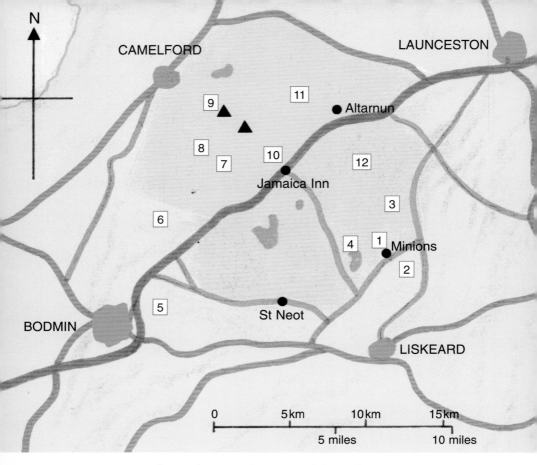

The approximate locations of the walks in this book

All the walks in this book were checked prior to printing, at which time
the instructions were correct. However, changes can occur in the
countryside over which we have no control. Please let us know
if you encounter any serious problems.

First published 2008 This reprint 2010
Bossiney Books Ltd, Langore, Launceston, Cornwall PL15 8LD
www.bossineybooks.com

ISBN 978-1-899383-81-8

Acknowledgements
The maps are by Graham Hallowell, the photographs by the author.
Cover based on a design by Heards Design Partnership

Printed in Great Britain by R Booth Ltd, Penryn, Cornwall

Introduction

These 'shortish' walks range from 4.5 to 9.4 km (2 3/4 to 5 3/4 miles) and typically take a couple of hours. The exact time will vary according to fitness, weather conditions, and above all how interested you are in what you see. The duration times given make no allowance for this, as it is such a variable: on most of these walks there is plenty of archaeological or historical interest, not to mention wildlife.

Safety (please take seriously but don't let it put you off!)

Bodmin Moor is not at a particularly high altitude, and it may not look that extensive on a map, but do not underestimate it. This is the first high ground the wind encounters after crossing the Atlantic, and if you experience bad weather here you will know you are indeed hill-walking.

The moor is also little used by other walkers, especially compared with Dartmoor. That is one of its delights, but also an extra reason why you need to go prepared. If you walk alone, be sure that someone knows where you are going; if you do have a problem, you may find your mobile phone gets no reception.

The weather can change abruptly. The 'low cloud' which spoils an afternoon on the beach can be experienced on the moor as fog. Apart from the risk of getting disorientated in what even in good weather is sometimes a featureless landscape, the temperature drops abruptly. Always take more layers of clothing than you expect to need, in addition to waterproofs, in your rucksack. Carry a supply of water with you (dehydration makes you tired) and some spare food. You need proper walking boots or shoes for grip and ankle support – and even after a month without rain (rare!) some parts of all these routes will be soggy underfoot.

I recommend you carry a compass for most of these walks as a safety measure: for some of them you will need it to follow the directions. And although, thanks to GPS, our sketch maps are fairly accurate for the actual route taken, if you do stray from the route they will be of limited use. You should take the OS Explorer sheet 109 for safety.

Bogs are a potential danger, and could even be lethal, especially after prolonged wet weather. The nineteenth century writer the Revd. Sabine Baring-Gould insisted that the bogs on Bodmin Moor were far worse than those on Dartmoor, and recounted how he had sunk to his armpits in what he called Redmire, but which is now called Redmoor Marsh (see map on page 30). He narrowly escaped, though with the loss of his gaiters and his dignity. If you find yourself beginning to enter a boggy area, return exactly the way you came, then find a way round the outside.

Paul White

A potted history of Bodmin Moor

The moor is one of a chain of granite outcrops extending from Dartmoor to Scilly. All have features in common, most obviously tors and granite quarries. But they share other features too. Around the edges of the granite outcrops, mineral lodes occur, in particular tin and copper ores, and most of the outcrops have a history of metal mining. Kaolin (china clay) is also associated with the fringes of granite outcrops. These industrial activities have all left their mark on the moorland landscapes.

Indeed, the marks of human activity on granite moorland, once made, tend to remain visible for a very long time. This is because the land is marginal, not of great agricultural value due to its poor soil and the harsh climate. It has only been intensively used during periods when the climate was drier and warmer than it is now (notably in the Bronze Age, around 2200-1000 BC, and from AD 800-1300) and when an expanding population put pressure on existing cultivated land, as happened both in the medieval period prior to the Black Death in 1348 and then again in the nineteenth century.

The remains of those three periods, Bronze Age, medieval and Victorian, litter the moor, especially the granite structures, simply because it has never been worth anyone's time to clear them away.

Although, during the Ice Ages, Cornwall was never covered by ice, it was not until around 6000 BC that stone-age hunter-gatherers started to come in any numbers. As the climate warmed, the land became thickly forested, but the moor was never fully covered. This may well have attracted early farmers, some time after 4000 BC, but they probably still lived mainly by hunting and the corralling of wild herds onto grazing land, with crop growing as a lesser activity.

It is possible that the hilltop enclosures on Roughtor and at Stowes Pound date from this period. They are now considered to be not forts but tribal meeting places or ritual centres. Long cairns and chambered tombs (notably Trethevy Quoit) date from much the same time. Stone rows and circles came rather later, perhaps around 2500-2000 BC, but no exact dates have been established.

Gradually – probably very gradually – people adopted a more settled lifestyle, and created field systems, interspersed with 'hut circles'. Not all the huts were homes, some were barns and sheds.

For those of us who walk the moors, the survival of so much visible evidence provides a fascinating insight into those ancient times, but for archaeologists the moors can be frustrating. The acid moorland soils have destroyed most of the evidence beyond what we can all see.

Archaeologists, however, are rather better than we are at identifying what is prehistoric and what is medieval. As a lay person's rule of thumb, most medieval buildings are rectangular whereas most prehistoric houses are round. On the other hand, Bronze Age field systems are often meticulously rectangular, whilst medieval fields may be higgledy-piggledy!

Bronze is an alloy of copper and tin, and it is possible (but unproven) that Cornish tin was extracted as far back as the Bronze Age. It is quite likely that 'farmers' were also tinners, in prehistory and certainly later. Tin ore was at first not mined, but sieved for. This developed into tin streaming, where the banks of suitable streams were dug away and sieved on a small industrial scale. Bodmin Moor used to be known as Foweymore, and around AD 1200 was the largest producer of tin in the south-west.

The next development was the digging of a series of pits along a lode, but actual shaft mining was a late development and required a lot of risk-capital investment. On the whole, Bodmin Moor did not merit this, until the copper boom of the 1830s which centred on Minions. A network of industrial railway tracks was constructed, taking ore and granite down to Liskeard and onward to the port of Looe. A preserved engine house at Minions has interesting displays about this industry.

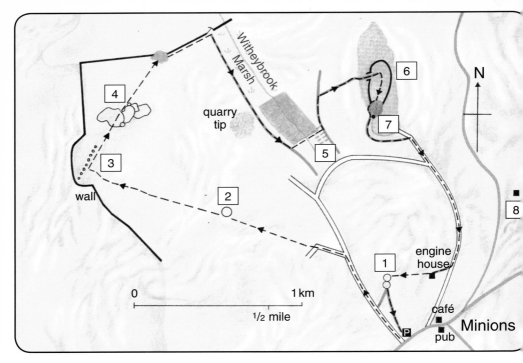

Walk 1   Minions, the Cheesewring side

Distance: 8 km (5 miles)   Time: 3 hours
Character: This walk has everything! Scenery, antiquities of several
kinds, and fascinating remains of mining and quarrying activities.
Some information is given on pages 8-9, and you will find much more
in the Minions Heritage Centre, in a preserved engine house.

Physically, the walk is undemanding except for the steep climb up
to Stowe's Pound and some rock clambering around the Cheesewring,
which could both be omitted. You will need a compass to follow the
directions. Old industrial areas like this can be dangerous – deep
quarry pools and hidden shafts do exist, so take care.

Start from the Hurlers Halt car park (SX 260711). Take the old industrial track from the car park entrance, passing on your right the
Hurlers (1) and their outlying stones.

After 650 m, branch left on a similar but less walked track, heading
west-north-west. Shortly, the track bends to the left. Leave it at this
point and continue west-north-west across grass, passing 20 m to the
right of a marker stone. With luck you will find another stone circle
(2). It isn't easy to spot, since the stones have all fallen. There is a bush

growing at its centre, and an ancient holloway passes it at a tangent.

Continue west-north-west, heading slightly to the left of Siblyback Farm on the far side of a valley. Cross an old leat at a point about 50 m from a wall on your left and continue until, just short of a boundary wall, you reach a stone row (3) running at right-angles.

Turn right along it and continue in the same direction after it ends – heading towards a rocky high point on the skyline. You will begin to pass through a prehistoric settlement with derelict field walls and a few hut circles (4). On reaching the rocky outcrop, turn right along a modern stone wall.

Follow the wall first up and then downhill till you come to a gate. At that point turn right along a path. Witheybrook Marsh is on your left. Pass a quarry tip on your right, then enclosed fields on your left. At the far end of the enclosure, turn left along the wall and cross the deep gully (5) which was once part of Witheybrook Mine.

On the far side of the gully, head for the left end of the rocky hill ahead of you and seek out a path that climbs through the bracken up to the ridge. The ridge is crowned by a massive prehistoric stronghold called Stowe's Pound (6) and you may well enter through a gateway which must have been extremely impressive when built, 5500 or more years ago.

When you reach the ridge, a very different view opens up across the farmlands to the east, with Dartmoor beyond. Climb up the ridge, then make your way carefully to the right of the summit, with a bit of clambering involved, and round to that emblem of Cornwall, the Cheesewring (7).

Now descend carefully with a wire fence on your left and follow the fence round the outside of the Cheesewring quarry. Descend to the track which runs to the quarry entrance. It's worth taking a look inside the quarry before returning along the track, which is a former tramway, heading towards the TV mast on Caradon Hill. On your left you will see the preserved engine house and buildings of Prince of Wales Shaft (8).

Reaching a gate, bear right away from the track to another preserved engine house, Houseman's Shaft, now the Minions Heritage Centre with useful displays. Then head due west across disturbed ground towards another engine house on the skyline, and you will find yourself at the Hurlers (1). From here, turn south and you will pick up one of the paths back to the car park.

Notes on Walk 1

Minions Village is the major walking centre for this part of the Moor and supports a café, a pub and a village shop. The café sells specialist books about the moor.

1. 'The Hurlers' consists of three stone circles, two of them with their stones re-erected, which form part of a ceremonial landscape similar to those on Dartmoor. To the west of the circles are several standing stones, which are part of the same complex. The name comes from a Puritan tradition first reported in 1610 that young men playing at hurling (a Cornish precursor of rugby) were turned to stone for playing on a Sunday.

2. The Craddock Moor stone circle remains undisturbed with its stones lying flat and partly buried. It is probably part of the same ceremonial complex as the Hurlers and the stone row.

3. The stone row is one of eight on the moor, a tenth of the number on Dartmoor. None of them is particularly imposing – though it is hard to understand why their very existence was unknown 30 years ago. The row points towards a small tor on the horizon and is at right angles to a line through the Hurlers and the Craddock Down circle. This is probably no accident.

4. A prehistoric settlement occupies the ground between the end of the stone row and the tor. It consists of field boundaries and a few hut

8

circles. It is quite likely that this settlement was not contemporaneous with the building of the stone rows and circles – perhaps dating back a mere 3500 years.

5. The 'Old Tin Dyke' is a gully created probably in the later Middle Ages by miners 'streaming' for tin. Later the Witheybrook Mine exploited the lode using shafts.

6. Stowe's Pound is thought to date from around 3500 BC, some 1500 years earlier than the stone circles and rows. (For comparison, the earliest Egyptian pyramid was built around 2700 BC.) It consists of massive walls with impressive gates, and within the enclosure are numerous bases cleared for huts. It is not known whether it was built for defence like a walled town, or as a religious or trading centre.

7. The Cheesewring is a naturally weathered granite tor, with a distinctive shape: a 'cheesewring' is a cider press. This tor towers over the Cheesewring Quarry which was worked from 1845 to 1917, when the railway on which it depended was closed.

8. The preserved engine house, seen in the photograph below, was part of Phoenix United Mine, one of the longest working mines in this area. Its various parts had worked under other names – the detailed history of Cornish mining ventures is very complex. Whilst sharing in the copper boom of around 1835-1855, Phoenix was able to revert to tin mining and survived until 1898. It was then restarted and the preserved engine house was built around 1910, and the mine struggled on into the 1920s.

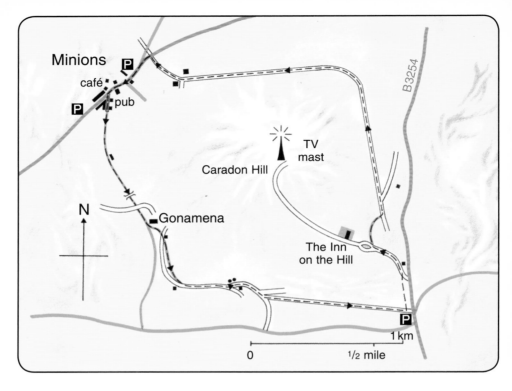

Walk 2   Caradon Hill

Distance: 7km (4¹/₄ miles)   Time: 2 hours
Character: An easy walk, much of it on old tramways. This area,
which is of great natural beauty, was the centre of a Victorian 'copper
boom'. The first part of the walk is a fascinating mixture of ruined
engine houses, spoil tips, devastation and a strange attraction – at least
in strong sunlight. Walk here in a mist and you might well see ghosts!

Warning: old mining areas are dangerous. We strongly recommend
that you stick to the paths and don't let children or dogs run loose.

Park at Minions, in the car park on the northern edge of the village
(SX262713). Walk to the centre of the village (see page 8). Just beyond
the Cheesewring Hotel, turn left along a track (PUBLIC FOOTPATH)
opposite Edgemoor Cottage. Continue through a small gate and along
an old industrial railway track. After several gates, duck under a low
bridge, pass through a cutting and cross a track onto a footpath.

    Cross a wooden stile and immediately turn left down a couple of
stone steps. Cross the valley, passing the Gonamena farmhouse, then

bear right to the remains of an engine house. Follow the track round the foot of a waste tip, soon bearing left onto a path which climbs slightly.

Follow the grassy path up and to the left as you pass another engine house, then join a track. Bear left between ruined mine buildings and stacks (shown in the photograph above) and continue on a broad track. Ignore the first track bearing off to the left, but follow the second, 25 m later.

Pass a waste tip, mostly on your left, and continue on the broad track to the road and car park at Tokenbury Corner, which is an alternative starting point.

Turn left parallel to the road, then left along a track behind buildings, which leads up to The Inn on the Hill, nestling in a plantation. About 100 m before the Inn, turn right past a tip, then down to join a former railway track which you can see running behind Caradon Villa. When it forks, take the upper track, which climbs at a gentle gradient for 2 km.

Pass between two engine houses and along an embankment. Descend to the road and turn left back to the start.

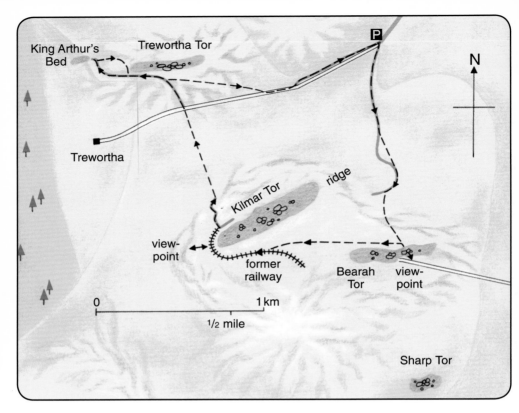

Walk 3 Kilmar Tor

Distance: 6.6 km (4 miles)   Time: 2 1/4 hours
Character: A walk in rugged granite terrain, with fairly gentle slopes
– but any number of tempting tors to climb if you really must! The
landscape and views are exceptional.

To get there, take the unsigned no-through-road from Berriow Bridge, on the Launceston to Liskeard road, B3254. Climb endlessly. Park just before the gate onto the moor, where there is room for half a dozen cars (SW 258759).

Go through the gate and bear left on the grassy track, initially with the wall on your left, then continuing ahead beyond the corner of the wall towards the ridge which extends left of Kilmar Tor. When the track divides, fork left. Reaching an old cart track, turn left and you will soon see the long ridge of Bearah Tor, with Sharp Tor beyond it.

Pass through a disused quarry, then turn left and head for the least rocky part of the Bearah ridge. Take your fill of the view from the

12

crest, then retrace your steps for 50m. Now head for the far left end of Kilmar Tor, passing its astonishing rock formations. After 750m you will notice the trackbed of the Kilmar Railway, built to carry granite from the quarries down to Looe, and closed in 1882. No need for wooden sleepers here.

Join the trackbed, which runs round the end of the Kilmar ridge – but divert out to see the view from its outpost, including the reconstructed Bronze Age village at Trewortha. Rejoin the trackbed, which soon peters out. Turn left down a fairly steep path.

Now make your way carefully north to the nearest point on the metalled track leading to Trewortha. The line you take is at a tangent to a great curving sweep of stone wall. Cross the track and follow the wall round, past Trewortha Tor and across some grassy ground to a (fairly) flat-topped tor known as King Arthur's Bed. If this really was King Arthur's bed, it is hardly surprising Guinevere left him for Lancelot, and a better knight's sleep.

As you return, take a look at the steep north side of Trewortha Tor, then cross to retrace your footsteps as far as the corner of the stone wall. Continue walking ahead from here, and in due course you will reach the track, which leads back to your car.

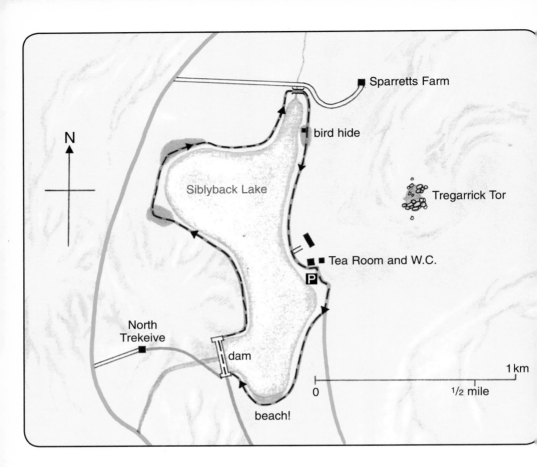

Walk 4 Siblyback Lake

Distance: 4.5km (2³/4 miles)   Time: 1¹/4 hours
Character: A very easy stroll along a permissive path, flat and mostly
even underfoot – an ideal starter walk if you are stressed, or out of
practice, or want to try out new boots!

Siblyback is a reservoir surrounded by low hills and tors, and is used
for sailing and fishing. It is very peaceful but (unusually for this book)
you are quite likely to meet other people walking.

Start from the car park (fee) or park on the road just before you reach
the car park. You can go round the lake in either direction, but I pre-
fer clockwise, arriving back at the Tea Room (seasonal opening). The
lakeside footpath starts just a few hundred metres back along the road
from the car park.

14

If this walk was not quite long enough for you, and you still feel energetic, you might like to try an additional walk – even shorter – in the woods at Golitha Falls, 1 km south-west of Siblyback Lake.

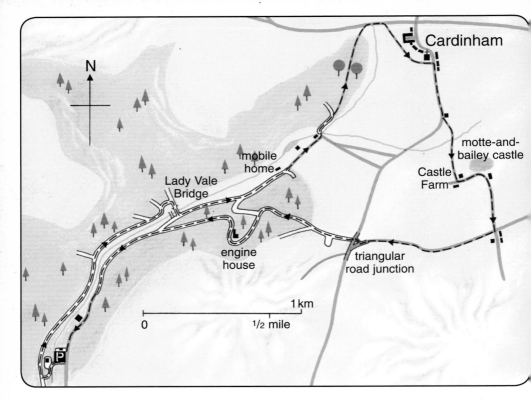

Walk 5 Cardinham Woods and village

Distance: 8.75 km (5¹/₂ miles)   Time: 2¹/₂ hours
*Character: Starts with attractive coniferous woods, then deciduous,
and farmland. An ancient 'road' leads to an early Norman castle and
the return goes back into the woodland, passing the remains of a mine.
Fairly easy walking: one long ascent on the short cut.*

Use the main car park at Cardinham Woods (SX100667) where there
are toilets, a café and picnic area. Cross the stream at the car park, pass
to the left of the children's play area and turn right up the valley on
LADY VALE WALK. At a major junction of tracks, turn right and right
again across the bridge (noting the clapper bridge alongside) then left
up the valley (WHEAL GLYNN). At the next junction, ignore the Wheal
Glynn turning.

Where the main track swings right, above a mobile home at the
time of writing, take the lesser track down to the left. It becomes a
lane. At a lane junction, turn left across the stream and follow the
main track up.

Turn right (yellow waymark) onto a path through a wood. Leave the wood by a stile and cross a field to a lane. Turn right, cross the stream and take the footpath on the right to the church. Don't miss the massive tenth century cross in the churchyard. Leaving the church, turn right along the lane for 400m to a steep hill sign.

You now have a choice. To take a short cut, continue along the road for a further kilometre, ignoring side turns, to a triangular road junction. Skip the next paragraph.

Or take the BRIDLEWAY signed to the left, but be warned – it can become very muddy indeed. Go through the yard of the house, then cross a streamlet (*not* over the little wooden bridge) and walk down beside it. This is clearly a very old 'road', leading across the valley to Castle Farm. Turn left here along the lane, and at the next bend you can just about see the fairly minimal remains of a motte-and-bailey castle, built about 1080. Continue up to the crossroads and turn right along the lane for 1 km, to a triangular road junction.

Ahead of you there are two tracks. Take the one on the right. (From the short cut, this is the first track on the right, just before the junction.) When it forks take the Forestry track bearing right. Follow the main track which at first winds downhill. At a fork bear left, slightly uphill. Near the head of a steep valley, you will pass the engine house of Hurstock Mine, where for a time in the 1850s silver was found as well as lead. The track rounds the head of the valley, then descends. Join the lower path and continue ahead to the car park

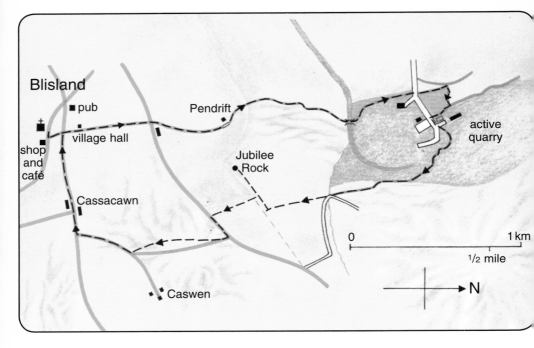

Walk 6 Blisland and the De Lank Quarries

Distance: 7km (4¼ miles) Time: 2 hours
Character: Starts at one of Cornwall's prettiest villages, with a shop,
a good pub, interesting church and (unusually for Cornwall) a village
green. Initially farming country with commonland, then a working
granite quarry. Footpaths and some quiet lanes. One steep descent, one
steep ascent, and some very uneven walking around the quarry area.
Take care when within the quarry, and stick to the path. A compass
will come in useful for directions.

Start from Blisland's church, St Protus and St Hyacinth. Take the road
up the side of the green (CASSACAWN/PENDRIFT) and at the crossroads
continue ahead up the lane past the village hall. At the next crossroads, continue ahead for PENDRIFT.

Cross a cattle grid, pass a house and go through a wooden gate.
Follow the yellow waymarks. The path descends steeply, then winds
across the valley floor to a footbridge. Cross the river and continue
following the waymarked path, first left along the bank then uphill.
Pass a house and cross the quarry access road, going through a kissing
gate. Now keep the fence on your right.

18

After 250 m, turn right across a stile. The path winds up to a junction. Turn right, and you will soon see the quarry on your left. Pick your way along the upper edge of the quarry, then descend to the quarry car park.

It is quite easy to miss your way here. Turn left (waymarked) past the settling tank. Then at the next waymark, take neither of the tracks but instead look for a narrow footpath bearing left (north-east). This winds up the hill to a stile. Turn right along the path. Go through a small gate, then through a field gate and turn right, keeping the hedge on your right. At a cattle grid and ford, use the stepping stones to the right, and continue up the slope ahead until (see map) you reach an old field boundary.

Turn right along it and with a bit of luck you will find the Jubilee Rock, a massive and rather bizarre celebration of the golden jubilee of George III in 1810. Retrace your steps to the corner of the enclosed land, then turn right (roughly south) till you reach a lane. Turn left, then at the next junction right. Walk parallel with the road, on the common land to the right. When you reach a cattle grid, walk down the lane to a T-junction and turn right, back to the village

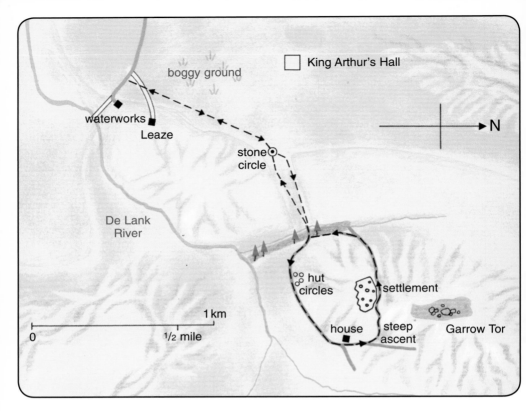

Walk 7 Garrow

Distance: 5.6km (3 1/2 miles)   Time: 1 1/2 hours
Character: The well preserved Bronze Age huts and medieval field
systems at Garrow make this one of the most evocative walks on the
moor, a great one to inspire children. For good measure, there is a
stone circle, and King Arthur's Hall if you have not already visited on
walk 8, with which this walk could be combined.

Park just short of the waterworks on Emblance Downs, beyond
Bolatherick (SX131767). Walk roughly north, keeping the enclosure
wall on your right until you reach a small stone circle. Walk uphill to
the stone wall ahead of you, and turn right along it.

Descend to a stile, then to a stream, walk through a conifer plantation, and then bear right uphill on an ancient trackway. As you climb
the slope you will begin to see some order in the scattered boulders.
They include the straight hedges of a field system at least medieval
in date. But as there are Bronze Age huts on the left of the path, it

is quite possible that the fields were laid out then and re-used in the Middle Ages.

Take your time exploring this remarkable site before continuing along the path and round a corner, when an impressive view of Brown Willy opens up ahead, with a permissive path on the right. There is a steep hill ahead, so you could retrace your steps if you want to avoid it. Otherwise continue past a house (shown in the photograph above) which at first sight may look deserted, but is not.

Bear left up a grassy path which winds to the crest of a ridge. You will see another enclosure on your left, with an old gateway. This too was once a settlement. If you are tempted to explore it, beware uneven ground and adders, for whom it is the perfect habitat.

Continue around the wall, then follow a rough path downhill towards the right end of the conifer plantation. Once on the flatter ground, bear left to join a path along the valley floor with the planta-tion on your right. Retrace your steps. You may want to visit King Arthur's Hall (see page 23). From there you need to walk one side or the other of the boggy ground directly between the Hall and your parking place.

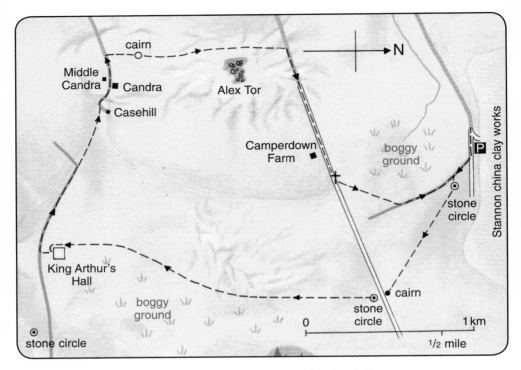

Walk 8   From Stannon to King Arthur's Hall

Distance: 8km (5 miles)   Time: 2¹/₄ hours
Character: Two fascinating ancient sites, and lovely scenery.
Open moorland: a compass is vital to follow directions and an OS
map for safety. Probably best as a dry weather walk, since parts could
become seriously boggy after prolonged rain.

To get there from Camelford, take the lane from Tregoodwell (at the
north end of the town) towards Roughtor, and turn right at a crossroads, ADVENT CHURCH. Keep left or turn left at all junctions, which
will ultimately bring you to Stannon china clay works (STANNON
HOUSE) where the tarmac stops. Park just beyond this (SX123801).

   Walk on up the track and after 100m bear right up a grassy track to
the Stannon stone circle, probably at least 4000 years old. Now head
roughly south-east (125° to be more precise) across open grassy moor.
You should in time reach a metalled track, with any luck near a cairn
on its north side. Head south from here and you will pass through
another stone circle, but this time the stones are fallen and you might
even miss it.

Continue to head roughly south across open moorland, trying as far as possible to use existing human and animal tracks and when in doubt diverting right rather than left, then after about 800m begin to veer to the right to avoid boggy ground (see sketch map). A strange fenced enclosure comes into view on the horizon, which looks rather like a reservoir, but is actually 'King Arthur's Hall'.

After exploring this site, head west to pick up a wall. Keep the wall on your left, ignore the stile to the left, and continue down to a lane. Follow it past Candra, and uphill until you reach open moor again. Turn right and head due north, passing the impressive remains of a concentric cairn, to head to the left of Alex Tor. Continue to a lane. Turn right along it and pass the enclosure of Camperdown Farm.

Reaching a medieval wayside cross, turn left onto the moor and head north-north-east, until you pick up a grassy track which leads you back to Stannon stone circle.

King Arthur's Hall

The only certainties about this site are that it is like no other ancient structure, and that it has nothing to do with King Arthur. Current orthodoxy says it is a medieval pound for illegally pastured livestock, but not everyone is convinced. It may be much more ancient, but has never been excavated so remains a mystery.

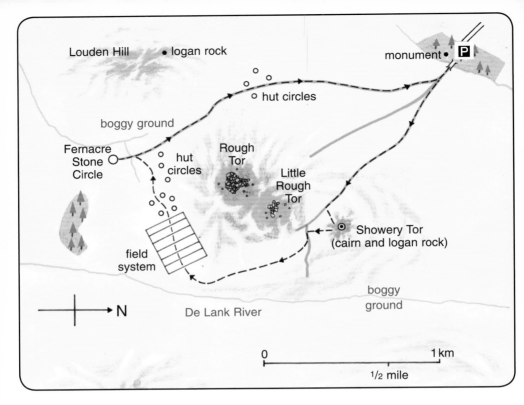

Louden Hill • logan rock monument • 🅿

hut circles

boggy ground

Fernacre Stone Circle hut circles

Rough Tor

Little Rough Tor

Showery Tor
(cairn and logan rock)

field system

boggy ground

→ N

De Lank River

0   1 km
                    ½ mile

Walk 9   A circuit of Rough Tor

Distance: 5.5 km (3½ miles)   Time: 1½ hours
Character: This walk combines great scenery with the remains of two Bronze Age villages and their ritual places. High moorland, so an OS map and a compass are recommended.

Start from the Roughtor car park (SX 138819) and descend to cross the stream. There are three rocky outcrops (tors) ahead of you. To the left of the main path is what looks like a curving stone wall, but is actually a cairn 500 m long, which was dug for a *Timeteam* programme in 2006 and found to be of Neolithic date (pre-2300 BC).

Take the grassy track which heads approximately between the tor on the left (the smallest, which is called Showery Tor) and the middle tor. Climb steadily uphill.

The track passes to the right of Showery Tor, but as you are abreast of it, turn left along a lesser path which leads to a strange rock formation, rather like the Cheesewring. Such piles occur naturally as the granite weathers – sometimes the top stone is a 'logan' or rocking stone.

This particular example is special, however, because a huge cairn was constructed around it, probably about 4000 years ago but perhaps as much as 5000, presumably because it had religious significance.

From Showery Tor you get a panorama, including across the valley to Brown Willy, Cornwall's highest point, and nearer to hand the ridge of Rough Tor.

Take the clear path towards Rough Tor, then divert to skirt around its left side, keeping between the granite boulders which litter its sides and the boggy ground of the De Lank river.

Continue in a south-west direction, heading roughly towards the right edge of a wood, about 2 km away. With luck you will find a path running at right angles to a succession of ancient field walls, but it can become obscured by bracken in summer. As you descend into the shallow valley of a stream (a bit boggy at its upper end) you should see the Fernacre stone circle on the far side (see photograph on page 1). Cross the stream to visit the circle.

Return across the stream and bear left, following a path or track along the side of the hill, and again passing numerous Bronze Age huts and field walls. You will see the car park slightly off to your left, above a plantation of conifers, but follow the indirect route of the track to avoid boggy ground.

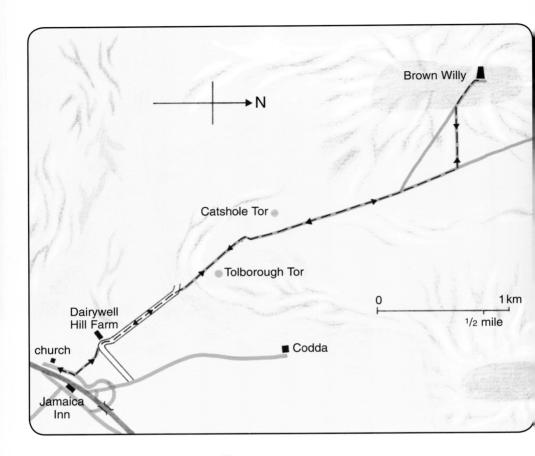

Walk 10   Brown Willy

Distance: 9.4km (5³/₄ miles)   Time: 3 hours

Character: At 420m Brown Willy is Cornwall's highest point, and it dominates the landscape of the moor like a mini-mountain. This walk involves a steep ascent and descent. It is a there-and-back walk (since any circular route would be too long to qualify as shortish) but if you enjoy moorland scenery you are unlikely to be disappointed on that account. It involves open moorland, and a map and compass are necessary for safety. This is access land but problems are occasionally reported, so please be prepared for minor changes to the route.

Park outside Bolventor church, which lies on the opposite side of the road from Jamaica Inn, so you will not have to go far for refreshments at the end of the walk.

Walk back up the road. Ignore the first footpath on your left, but take the second. Cross the field and follow the waymarks. At the foot of the slope turn left, to a stile, and take the track into Dairywell Hill farm. Walk up the track to the right of the farm, through two gates and onto the open moor.

Continue in the same direction, leaving the track when it veers away, and head north-west. Brown Willy suddenly comes into view. Continue north-west, joining a faint but broad grassy track which leads to a gate in the corner. Go through and turn left, keeping the wire fence on your left. Mostly this path runs between the fence and a hedge, but when it narrows you can walk along the top of the hedge, till it broadens again.

Whilst it is possible to cross the fence where barbed wire is missing, and take a short cut, there are good environmental reasons for sticking to the main route so please continue until you reach a stile on your left.

Cross the stile and approach the steep slope ahead, take a deep breath and climb to the summit, where the views will repay you for the effort.

Then return by the same route.

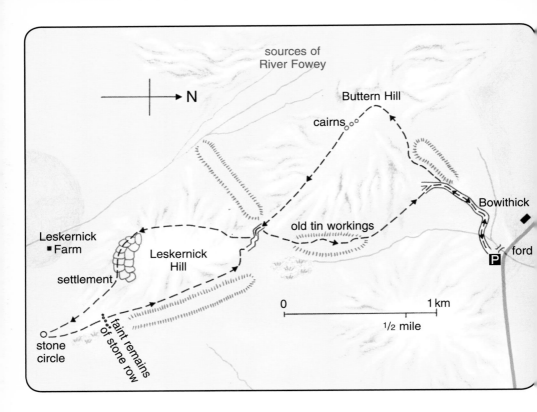

Walk 11 Leskernick Hill from Bowithick

Distance: 8km (5 miles)   Time: 2 1/2 hours
Character: Open moorland with extensive views and few (if any)
other walkers. You will need a compass to follow the directions, and a
map for safety. Bronze Age features include cairns, a stone circle and
a village site, and there is some quite dramatic evidence of nineteenth
century tin extraction. One steep ascent, but otherwise fairly easy
walking.

Park off-road near Bowithick, beside a ford and a ruined bridge
(SX 183826). Walk south-west up the track (noting Buttern Hill ahead
of you, which you are about to climb) to a gate at the foot of a worked-
out tin stream.

Leave the track and continue uphill with the tin stream on your
right. Make your way to the summit, where you will find ancient
cairns, one with a cist or stone coffin, not to mention a fabulous view
over most of the moor.

From the summit, take a course almost south-east – on a clear day, aim for the TV transmitter mast in the distance.

Then head down to the obvious crossing point over the streamwork ahead, cross over and head due south, uphill. Skirt round to the right of the summit and you will find the remains of a Bronze Age field system and, if you are very lucky, a hut circle. Walk south-east from the settlement and try to locate the remains of a stone circle, perhaps contemporary with the settlement, but probably even older.

From the circle, head north, keeping to the left of old workings, and crossing the faint remains of a stone row. Climb gently to skirt Leskernick Hill on your left, and deep streamworks on your right. With an obviously boggy area ahead of you, swing slightly left and descend to cross the streamworks on the track you used before.

Once across, turn right and make your way along the valley with the stream on your right, passing through mining remains. Keep to the left of a wire fence till you reach a track, which leads back to your starting point.

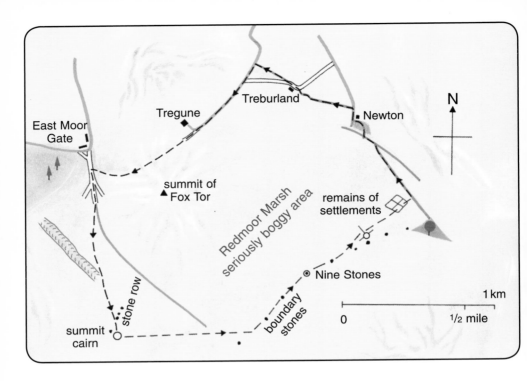

Walk 12 East Moor

Distance: 7.25 km (4¹/₂ miles)   Time: 2¹/₂ hours
Character: Open moorland, very lonely, then a return along the
moorland edge. You pass a stone row, a stone circle, and an ancient
settlement. This is quite a difficult route for navigation. You will need
a compass to follow the directions, and an OS map for safety. It is a
landscape without many landmarks, so choose a really clear day.

Start from East Moor Gate (SX 222790). When parking, please don't
obstruct gateways, passing places, or residents' access. Go through the
gate onto the open moor. Start by following the track ahead then head
due south for 1 km to the summit of a low rounded hill. The OS map
shows various archaeological features, of which the summit ring-cairn
is easy to see, and several stones at the top of the stone row.

   From the summit cairn, head due east for 800 m and keep a good
lookout for a row of boundary markers. Many of them have fallen,
especially to the south-western end, so they are hard to spot. Turn left,
north-east, along the row, which leads to an attractive stone circle, the
Nine Stones, and then beyond, over the top of a ridge. If the bracken

is low, you will see evidence of field walls and buildings, perhaps 3500 years old. Continue in the same direction downhill. Aim about 100 m to the left of the walled wood and you will find further remains of a substantial settlement. (On two occasions when the climate changed for the worse – around 1000 BC and again around AD 1300 – farms on the high ground were abandoned. The modern farms, mostly with 'Tre-' names, probably date from around AD 900-1200, though obviously the buildings are not that old.)

If the bracken is high you will not see the field system. The clear routes down through the bracken vary slightly from from year to year, but head for the walled wood, then skirt its left side, down to a wall. Turn left and follow a path with the wall on your right. When the wall ends, continue ahead down a rough track as waymarked.

After 250 m, bear left on a track above a wood. (This track also serves as a watercourse!) After 40 m, turn right over a stile into and through the wood. Emerging from the wood, turn sharp left to a stile, then right along the lane. After 100 m, turn left on PUBLIC FOOTPATH. After about 300 m cross a stream and climb up to Treburland farm. Walk ahead on the farm track, then take the footpath on the right over a high stile, and cross the field diagonally left.

A stile leads to a lane. Turn left up the lane, which continues as a track to a moor gate. Keep the wall on your right and make your way over tussocky ground back to East Moor Gate.

Access Land and responsible walking

Until the so-called 'right-to-roam' legislation (the C.R.O.W. Act) it was very difficult to suggest really good legal walks on Bodmin Moor, since rights-of-way were scarce and did not combine to make good off-road walking.

Every single walk in this book depends in part on Access Land.

Landowners are entitled, on giving good reasons and subject to notice, to close their land temporarily. For most of these walks, we think such closure is unlikely to occur, but we apologise if it does. You can check on this government website if you are concerned:

www.countrysideaccess.gov.uk/things_to_do/open_access

Bodmin Moor may look like a wilderness, but it is actually a managed agricultural landscape. Neither landowners nor conservationists are entirely happy with 'right-to-roam', and both parties have real reason for concern. Moorland may look robust, but heather and bogs are fragile environments.

Please stick to paths (human and animal) wherever possible, even if this means following a slightly winding route. If the directions take you on a compass course across open moorland (other than grass) please don't just identify a distant point and charge across with your eyes on the horizon! Look where you are walking and tread carefully. If an area is fenced off for regeneration or special protection, please accept that there is probably a very good reason.

All the old rules in the 'Countryside Code' still apply, but we assume our readers know about gates and not picking flowers or leaving litter!

Dog-walking

There are legal restrictions on dog-walkers within Access Land. You must use a short lead when near livestock, and everywhere between 1 March and 31 July, which is the ground-nesting bird season. Even outside that time-span, please keep your dogs under close control.

Some other Bossiney Walks Books

Shortish walks in north Cornwall (5-8 km walks)
Shortish walks near the Land's End (5-8 km walks)
Shortish walks on and around The Lizard (4-9 km walks)
Shortish walks – Truro to Looe (5-9 km walks)
Shortish walks St Ives to Padstow (5-8 km walks)
Shortish walks on Dartmoor (5-8 km walks)